"The Earth Does Not Belong To Man"

Conservation Poems

by Judith Nicholls and others

For Lucy, Kevin, Alex and Louisa Ding, with love.

Contents

Section 1

Slick Monster	2
What Is One?	3
The Dodo	4
Rainforest Song	6
Sealsong	8
Circus Elephant	8
Names	9
What On Earth?	10

Section 2

Tree Song	11
The Intruder	11
Spaceship Earth	12
Song in Space	13
The Song of the Whale	14
Weep with the Whale	15
Take One Home for the Kiddies	16
Slow Worm	17

Section 3

This Letter's To Say	18
Earth Riddles	20
The Whale	21
The Trunk	22
Future Past	24
The Elephant Table	26
Harvest Hymn	28
Mummy, Oh Mummy	30
The Lost Angels	32

"The earth does not belong to man; man belongs to the earth."
Chief Seattle

Edinburgh Gate
Harlow, Essex

Slick Monster

Velvet black wave
gently laps the shore;
small white seagull
flies no more.

Shiny black monster
slowly creeps to land;
small pink crab
buried in the sand.

        Judith Nicholls

What Is One?

One is the sun,
a rhino's horn;
a drop of dew,
a lizard's tongue.

One is the world,
a lonely whale;
an elephant's trunk,
a monkey's tail.

One is an acorn,
one is a moon;
one is a forest,
felled too soon.

Judith Nicholls

The Dodo

The Dodo used to walk around,
And take the sun and air.
The sun yet warms his native ground –
The Dodo is not there!

The voice which used to squawk and squeak
Is now for ever dumb –
Yet may you see his bones and beak
All in the Mu-se-um.

                    Hilaire Belloc

Rainforest Song

(for the people)

Forest, my mother,
feed me your fruit.
Forest, my father,
trace me my root.
Forest, my shelter,
spread me your shade,
as I walk in the glow
of your green forest glade.

Forest of whispers
and intricate ways,
Forest of spirits
that slip through your maze,
Forest of mystery,
subtle and deep,
you glide like a snake
through my waking and sleep.

Forest, the home
of my eye and my hand,
Forest, the meaning
I understand,
Forest, the ground
where I place my tread,
where I breathe my being
and pillow my head,

Forest, the world
I depend upon,
where will I walk
when my Forest has gone?

Tony Mitton

Sealsong

Around me, seas
stretch endlessly;
above me, sky.
A space to breathe,
a place to swim;
to pace the days
by moon or sun.
A place that time
had kept from man;

no place to die.

                Judith Nicholls

Circus Elephant

Today, I dance,
I tiptoe, sway,
with sawdust at my knees;
yesterday, lifetimes away,
I lumbered through the trees.

                Judith Nicholls

Names

My name is "Couldn't care less",
just let the forests die.
My name is "Can't be bothered",
who cares about holes in the sky?

My name is "I'm too busy",
let someone else do the worrying,
there's nothing that I can do
if the ice caps are wearing thin.

My name is "Leave me alone",
just don't go preaching to me.
Gossip is what I care about
not oil that's spilt in the sea.

My name is "I'm alright Jack",
there's really no cause for alarm.
Hens are silly birds, who cares
if they suffer at the factory farm?

Who cares about global warming,
I like a spot of hot weather.
My name is "Sit on the fence",
my name is "All of a dither".

So stop saying what I should think,
I don't want to believe what I'm told.
My name is "Hope it will go away",
My name is "Don't get involved".

And who do you think you are,
telling us all we should worry?
WELL, MY NAME'S A WARNING
 FROM FUTURE YEARS,
IT'S "LISTEN OR YOU'LL BE SORRY".

Brian Moses

What On Earth?

What on earth are we doing?
Once wood-pigeons flew,
and young badgers tunnelled
where oak and ash grew …

Now, the forest's a runway,
and all that flies through
is a whining grey plane
where the pigeons once flew.

Where on earth are we going?
At the end of the lane
once blackberries hung
in soft autumn rain …

Now the lane is a car park,
and never again
will fruit fill our baskets
down in the lane.

Why on earth are we crying?
Once morning dew shone
on hawthorn and primrose,
caught in the sun …

Now the forest is carpeted
only with stone.
No primrose, no hawthorn;
the forest has gone.

Judith Nicholls

Tree Song

City of whispers,
symphony of sighs,
intricate embroidery
sampling the skies.

Machinery of nature,
factory of air,
delirious dancer
dishevelling her hair.

Tony Mitton

The Intruder

Two-boots in the forest walks,
Pushing through the bracken stalks.

Vanishing like a puff of smoke,
Nimbletail flies up the oak.

Longears helter-skelter shoots
Into his house among the roots.

At work upon the highest bark,
Tapperbill knocks off to hark.

Painted-wings through sun and shade
Flounces off along the glade.

Not a creature lingers by,
When clumping Two-boots comes to pry.

James Reeves

Spaceship Earth

I am …

space-dancer,
drawn to the light like a moth;

an ancient coin
spun through night air;

silver penny,
lost in a deep pocket;

small change,
cast on a dark cloth –
a wager on life …

*Spend me
if you dare!*

Judith Nicholls

Song in Space

When man first flew beyond the sky
He looked back into the world's blue eye.
Man said: What makes your eye so blue?
Earth said: The tears in the ocean do.
Why are the seas so full of tears?
Because I've wept so many thousand years.
Why do you weep as you dance through space?
Because I am the Mother of the Human Race.

Adrian Mitchell

The Song of the Whale

Heaving mountain in the sea,
Whale, I heard you
Grieving.

Great whale, crying for your life,
Crying for your kind, I knew
How we would use
Your dying:

Lipstick for our painted faces,
Polish for our shoes.

Tumbling mountain in the sea,
Whale, I heard you
Calling.

Bird-high notes, keening,
Soaring:
At their edge a tiny drum
Like a heartbeat.

We would make you
Dumb.

In the forest of the sea,
Whale, I heard you
Singing.

Singing to your kind.
We'll never let you be.
Instead of life we choose

Lipstick for our painted faces,
Polish for our shoes.

Kit Wright

Weep with the Whale

The great grey bodies
swing and twist with
slow grace, like Olympic
gymnasts in an action
    replay.

Their songs are the
mournful mouth-music
of the deep, pitched
thin and high with
    sadness.

Joined in an underwater
ceilidh, their keening
echoes on the waves
like a lament for the
    future.

Moira Andrew

Take One Home for the Kiddies

On shallow straw, in shadeless glass,
Huddled by empty bowls, they sleep:
No dark, no dam, no earth, no grass –
Mam, get us one of them to keep.

Living toys are something novel,
But it soon wears off somehow.
Fetch the shoebox, fetch the shovel –
Mam, we're playing funerals now.

                                 Philip Larkin

Slow Worm

It needed a home,
this intriguing new pet.
What could I provide?
Earth, a stone,
grass, some bark?
Somewhere for it to hide.

Sleek, lithe,
like a miniature snake
with tiny black bead eyes …
I placed some turf
in a cardboard box,
thinking that would suffice.

Within a few days
I sensed its distress,
this creature full of grace.
Shame crept in,
I knew deep down
it needed far more space.

I set it down
in the garden,
bravely watched it glide
in and out
through blades of grass.
I felt a sense of pride.

Tracey Blance

This Letter's To Say

Dear Sir or Madam,
This letter's to say
Your property
Stands bang in the way
Of Progress, and
Will be knocked down
On March the third
At half-past one.

There is no appeal,
Since the National Need
Depends on more
And still more Speed,
And this, in turn,
Dear Sir or Madam,
Depends on half England
Being tar-macadam.
(But your house will –
We are pleased to say –
Be the fastest lane
Of the Motorway).

Meanwhile the Borough
Corporation
Offer you new
Accommodation
Three miles away
On the thirteenth floor
(Flat Number Q
6824).

But please take note,
The Council regret:
No dog, cat, bird
Or other pet;
No noise permitted,

No singing in the bath
(For permits to drink
Or smoke or laugh
Apply on Form
Z 327);
No children admitted
Aged under eleven;
No hawkers, tramps,
Or roof-top lunchers;
No opening doors
To Bible-punchers.

Failure to pay
Your rent, when due,
Will lead to our
Evicting you.
The Council demand
That you consent
To the terms above
When you pay your rent.

Meanwhile we hope
You will feel free
To consult us
Should there prove to be
The slightest case
Of difficulty.

With kind regards,
Yours faithfully …

   Raymond Wilson

Earth Riddles

Painted glass bauble,
swung on an unseen thread.

Curled palette of light,
splashed on dark canvas.

Lapis lazuli,
brush-stroked with white.

Lone marble,
rolled over threadbare velvet.

A medal,
pinned to the blue blazer of night.

Space-hopper,
cast like a kite over silent seas.

Small change
in a deep pocket.

Judith Nicholls

The Whale

Pity the poor whale –
She is nothing at all
But nostrils and an enormous lung.
She feeds cold milk to her young.
Nevertheless, piecemeal,
She builds a whale
Nest on the ocean bed
For each huge sleepyhead.
Beneath her move
Crustaceous depths, above
The celestial foam,
The wake of liners steaming home.

John Mole
(adapted from the French
of Robert Desnos)

The Trunk

Above crisp packets,
Cans of Coke, and ice-creams,
Using a finger with sixty
Thousand muscles, a mountain seems

To be looking for something;
Not just for twig ends,
The soft bark of young trees,
And the salt-lick that sends

Minerals to feed its mind,
But something beyond the sea
Of faces, the jungle
Of towerblocks; that we

Can't throw over a wall
Or through gaps in a cage,
Because this isn't a finger
Like ours that searches a page,

Or a vacuum cleaner
That sucks up any old junk:
This is an elephant looking
For Africa with its trunk.

John Lynch

Future Past

Lord of Africa,
swaying giant of the plains;
tree-mover,
sand-tosser,
diviner of water
from the dry river bed:
where are you now?

Where is the song on ivory keys
that echoed through the dusk?
The song's cut away
for a handful of beads
which once were a living tusk.
Now only baubles
glint in the sun,
for the forest lord fell
to the sound of a gun.

     Judith Nicholls

The Elephant Table

Grandma boot-polished them
    glistening black –
four mahogany heads
facing north, south, east, west
    with a world on their back,

a world carved out whole
    from one slice of a tree,
a world that grew old
while the Viceroy asked princes
    to treaties and tea

and outside in the dust
    quiet lean watchful men
and their elephants waited
what seemed like an age
    for the party to end.

In Grandma's dark parlour
    I crouched eye to eye
with the south-facing elephant.
Where was it looking
    so weary, and why?

And what makes me reach back
    years later to feel
little-finger-sized tusks?
"Those are precious," said Grandma.
    "They're real."

Philip Gross

Harvest Hymn

We plough the fields and scatter
our pesticides again;
our seeds are fed and watered
by gentle acid rain.
We spray the corn in winter
till pests and weeds are dead –
who minds a little poison
inside his daily bread?

*All good gifts around us
beneath our ozone layer
are safe, oh Lord,
so thank you Lord
that we know how to care.*

Judith Nicholls

Mummy, Oh Mummy

"Mummy, Oh Mummy, what's this pollution
That everyone's talking about?"
"Pollution's the mess that the country is in,
That we'd all be far better without.
It's factories belching their fumes in the air,
And the beaches all covered with tar,
Now throw all those sweet papers into the bushes
Before we get back in the car."

"Mummy, Oh Mummy, who makes pollution,
And why don't they stop if it's bad?"
"'Cos people like that just don't think about others,
They don't think at all, I might add.
They spray all the crops and they poison the flowers
And wipe out the birds and the bees,
Now there's a good place we could dump that old mattress
Right out of sight in the trees."

"Mummy, Oh Mummy, what's going to happen
If all the pollution goes on?"
"Well the world will end up like a second-hand junk-yard,
With all of its treasures quite gone.
The fields will be littered with plastics and tins,
The streams will be covered with foam,
Now throw those two pop bottles over the hedge,
Save us from carting them home."

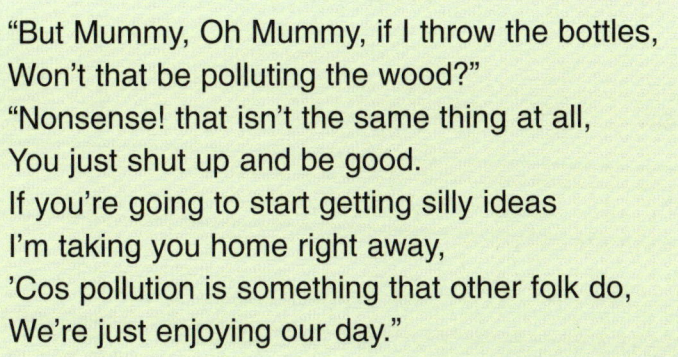

"But Mummy, Oh Mummy, if I throw the bottles,
Won't that be polluting the wood?"
"Nonsense! that isn't the same thing at all,
You just shut up and be good.
If you're going to start getting silly ideas
I'm taking you home right away,
'Cos pollution is something that other folk do,
We're just enjoying our day."

Anon.

The Lost Angels

In a fish tank in France
we discovered the lost angels,
fallen from heaven and floating now
on imaginary tides.
And all along the sides of the tank,
faces peered, leered at them,
laughing, pouting,
pointing, shouting,
while hung above their heads, a sign,
"Ne pas plonger les mains dans le bassin,"
Don't put your hands in the tank
– the turtles bite seriously.
And who can blame them,
these creatures with angels' wings,
drifting past like alien craft.
Who knows what signals they send
through an imitation ocean,
out of sight of sky,
out of touch with stars?

Dream on, lost angels,
then one day, one glorious day,
you'll flap your wings
and fly again.

Brian Moses